Niagara-on-the-Lake

Niagara-on-the-Lake

Cosmo Condina

Whitecap Books

North Vancouver ● British Columbia ● Canada

Canadian Cataloguing in Publication Data

Condina, Cosmo.
    Niagara-on-the-Lake

ISBN 0-920620-53-1

1. Niagara-on-the-Lake (Ont.) — Description —
Views. 2. Historic buildings — Ontario —
Niagara-on-the-Lake — Pictorial works. I. Title.
FC3099.N5C66 1984   917.13'51   C84-091181-5
F1059.5.N5C66 1984

Designed by Michael E. Burch
Printed by D. W. Friesen & Sons Ltd.
Altona, Manitoba

© **Whitecap Books Ltd.**
1086 W. 3rd Street
North Vancouver, B.C., Canada

First Edition 1984

Printed in Canada

Foreword by the Deputy Premier of Ontario
The Honourable Robert Welch, Q.C., M.P.P.

1984 marks the Province of Ontario's Bicentennial. Two hundred years ago the major migration of loyalists and other settlers arrived on the shore of Lake Ontario. Faced with many obstacles and hardships, this group formed a strong nucleus which grew until in 1867, Ontario and its people entered the Canadian Confederation as important participants. During the two centuries since 1784, this initial migration has been joined by thousands of other people, from all parts of the world, to form a strong multicultural and multifaceted Province, yet with a unity of purpose and dedication committed to continuing the building of a great country.

Communities are important in Ontario. Indeed, many of the settlements which began during the 1784 migration grew into the major centres of today. The people of Ontario focus their attention on many important things. One major focus has always been one's community.

One such community is Niagara-on-the-Lake, and it is this community that one of its residents, Cosmo Condina, has focused on through his camera lens. He has captured, through his talents, the many facets of Niagara, its rich history, its link with land and water, and its beauty.

Actually, Niagara-on-the-Lake got the jump on the rest of the Province's Bicentennial celebrations when it marked the two-hundredth anniversary of the commencement of settlement in the Niagara area in 1981. As the fall-out from the American Revolutionary War was felt, many soldiers loyal to the cause of Britain moved to the Niagara area in 1781, in order to escape reprisals and live under the Crown.

Niagara was important to North American Indian history before this time, though. During the 1600's, the entire Niagara Peninsula was the home of the Neutral Indians, who were caught in the middle of the Iroquois to the south, and the Hurons to the north, Indian nations which were enemies for years. The Neutrals, as the name implies, took no sides, allowing both armies to travel through their territory. After the Iroquois, of what became New York State, defeated the Hurons around 1650, they attacked and completely destroyed the Neutrals in a savage war which took place on the fields, and what would become the vineyards and orchards, of Niagara. The Seneca Iroquois, part of the Iroquois Five Nations, then took over the control of the Peninsula. In fact, the name 'Niagara' comes from the attempted French translation of the Indian name of the area, 'Onguiaahra'.

Samuel de Champlain's Indian agent, Etienne Brule, most probably was the first white man to visit the Neutrals' area in 1615. The French explorer La Salle, obsessed with trying to reach China via the Great Lakes and Mississippi River, sent Father Louis Hennepin into the area in 1678. Father Hennepin was most likely the first white man to view Niagara Falls. La Salle arrived in the Niagara area in early 1679, and, on the east bank of the Niagara River, where it empties into Lake Ontario, built Fort Conde, with the permission of the Iroquois. Fort Niagara was built on this site in 1725 by the French to control what was becoming a highly-developed trading route into the North American interior, which saw raw furs and agricultural products head east in return for finished goods from Montreal and Europe.

In 1759, the British finally took control of Fort Niagara from the French and a year later consolidated their hold over the rest of France's North American possessions. When the American Revolution broke out in 1776, Fort Niagara was a fully-developed British outpost and remained so until 1789, when it was turned over to the United States.

By that time, as has been hinted at earlier, a settlement on the west bank of the Niagara River at Lake Ontario, where Niagara-on-the-Lake now stands, had been in existence for about eight years. British soldiers and the loyalist Butlers' Rangers unit moved across the River. Political, administrative and judicial systems had to be developed in Upper Canada, and the west bank Niagara settlement, now called Newark, became the first seat of government in the Province. The Crown's representative in Upper Canada, Lieutenant-Governor John Graves Simcoe, opened the Province's first Parliament in 1792, with a small dose of pomp and ceremony, given the frontier nature of the capital.

Newark's prominence as Upper Canada's capital was not to last, however. Britain and the United States eyed each other with uneasy and suspicious glances, and finally, fearing the possible con-sequences of the capital's proximity to the United States, the seat of government and administration was moved across Lake Ontario to York, now Toronto.

The uneasy glances broke out into open warfare in 1812, and the United States and the infant provinces of Upper and Lower Canada fought an intense two-year struggle on a number of fronts, one of them being the Niagara Frontier. Some key battles were fought in the Niagara area, among them, Queenston Heights where Sir Isaac Brock died, and Lundy's Lane, where the battlefield was literally soaked with blood. Legends grew up around the roles and sacrifices of members of Niagara militia.

The war ended in 1814 and the Town of Niagara and surrounding area entered a period of peace, lasting to this day, interrupted only by the global wars of 1914-1918 and 1939-1945, to which its citizens went off to participate, and when the Canadian armed forces used Niagara as a training ground.

Between 1814 and the late 1830's, Niagara retained its importance as a training base and transshipment point on the Great Lakes-Niagara route established by the French one hundred years earlier. However, two canal systems, one American (the Erie) and one Canadian (the Welland) effectively ended this aspect of Niagara's commercial significance.

The Niagara area's importance as an agricultural centre grew, however. As more land was cleared in the Township areas settlers found a very fertile soil which initially caused crops such as wheat to thrive. Later the moderating effects of Lake Ontario, and a new generation of experimenting immigrants, led to the cultivation of tender fruit orchards and vineyards.

The Town of Niagara itself moved into an era at the mid to end of the nineteenth century as a holiday and cultural oasis. Many rich families built large estate homes. Stately churches to minister to the spiritual needs were constructed. Hotels, some not presently standing, were filled by affluent tourists arriving by rail or water. The Town, perhaps foreshadowing its importance eighty years later as the home of the Shaw Festival, became a Canadian home for the Chautauqua cultural, educational, and spiritual experience. An area at the western end of the Old Town is still called the Chautauqua region, so named after the festival.

As Niagara moved into the decades of the Twentieth Century, its agricultural importance grew, its cultural and recreational significance remained and, as the automobile arrived on the scene, it became a residential centre for people working in industries and trades connected with agriculture at Niagara, and for people whose jobs took them to larger centres at St. Catharines and Niagara Falls.

The mid and latter decades of the Twentieth Century have seen major developments. Interested individuals founded an annual festival around the plays of George Bernard Shaw. The opening of the Shaw Festival Theatre in 1973 led to a renaissance in Niagara-on-the-Lake in terms of culture, tourism and national recognition. Four years earlier, in 1969, the townships and urban areas of Niagara were amalgamated into the Town of Niagara-on-the-Lake. And commerce has not been forgotten either, with industries such as recreational boatbuilding, aircraft parts manufacturing and cottage wine-making joining tourism and culture as major contributors to Niagara-on-the-Lake's economic well-being.

Cosmo Condina has captured the pride, the heritage, and the celebration of Niagara-on-the-Lake in his photographs. As you turn the pages of this book, I think you will gain a sense of being in Niagara-on-the-Lake, of experiencing its charm, grandeur and natural beauty. You will see where Niagara-on-the-Lake finds itself two hundred-plus years after its birth, and why its people, while proud of its past, are excited and optimistic about its future.

The Honourable Robert Welch, Q.C., M.P.P.
Deputy Premier of Ontario
Niagara-on-the-Lake
January 1984

St. Mark's Anglican Church

One of the earliest Anglican churches in Ontario, St. Mark's Church was begun in 1804 to serve a congregation organized twelve years earlier. Among its parishioners were Lieutenant-Governor John Simcoe, Lieutenant-Colonel John Butler, and Major General Isaac Brock. The church, completed in 1810, was used as a hospital in 1812 and by the Americans as barracks in 1813. Burnt by the latter, the nave was rebuilt by 1822. In 1843 the structure was altered by the addition of the transepts, chancel and the present Gothic Revival pulpits. Further interior alterations were made in 1892 and 1964.

Spring brings glorious displays of blossoms for travellers along the Niagara Parkway.

Early blooming crocuses along the Niagara Parkway.

The Stewart-McLeod House, circa 1830, a typical example of late Georgian architecture.

The Clench House, built in the 1820s by an officer of Butler's Rangers.

Laura Secord House

Laura Ingersoll Secord (1775-1868) was born in Great Barrington, Massachusetts, and came to Upper Canada with her father in 1795 to settle in this area. About two years later she married James Secord, a United Empire Loyalist, and within seven years they had moved to this site from nearby St. Davids. From here during the War of 1812, Laura Secord set out on an arduous 19-mile journey to warn the local British commander, a Lieutenant James Fitzgibbon, of an impending American attack. The courage and tenacity displayed on this occasion in June 1813 placed her in the forefront of the province's heroines. Mrs. Secord's house, a simple frame building, was restored (1971-72) and remains as a memorial to this exceptional act of patriotism.

The natural beauty of the area around Niagara-on-the-Lake, in conjunction with its warm summer climate, make this one of the most beautiful areas of Canada. In spring the gardens come alive after the deep hibernation of winter, and the many thousands of fruit trees provide a spectacular show of blossoms, promising a rich summer harvest.

The Niagara Apothecary

    The Niagara Apothecary building (c. 1820s) opened its doors as an Apothecary in 1866. It is the only surviving Confederation-period building in Niagara-on-the-Lake. The interior was decorated much as it is at present and the Florentine windows imparted Italian-design detail to the handsome mid-Victorian front. The interior fittings, dating from 1866, were still in use in 1964 when the last proprietor, E. W. Field, one of the only six pharmacist-owners closed the pharmacy that year because of ill health.

    In July 1969 the Ontario Heritage Foundation acquired the building. The restoration, by noted restoration architect Peter J. Stokes, is regarded as one of the finest and most authentic in North America. The Niagara Apothecary was dedicated May 14, 1971, and is operated by the Ontario College of Pharmacists as a pharmacy museum.

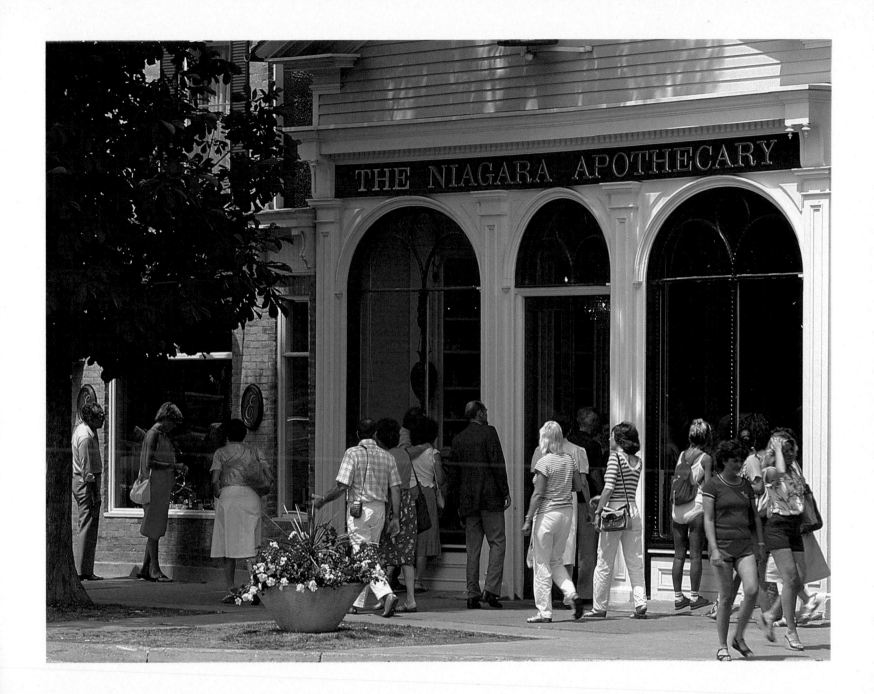

The setting sun casts a gentle glow over the spacious grounds of Letchworth.

The Richardson-Kiely House, circa 1832.

Niagara Historical Society Museum

This building, the first in Ontario to be constructed for use solely as an historical museum, was begun in 1906 and completed the following year. Its erection was due largely to the dedicated efforts of Miss Janet Carochan, founder, and for thirty years, curator of the Niagara Historical Society. Donations were received from the Federal and Provincial Governments, local municipalities, British Regiments once stationed in the area, and private citizens. Displays and room settings reflect Pioneer Settlement, United Empire Loyalists and Victoriana period. A special collection from the families of William Kirby, Laura Secord and Daniel Servos are present.

Town Clock

On June 28, 1920 a public referendum decided whether a plain monument, construction of a new school, a recreation area, a modern hospital or the Town Clock would be used as a tribute to the Town's War dead. The Town Clock was overwhelmingly chosen, and it was unveiled June 23, 1922. The names of the Town dead from World War II were added in 1947. It is interesting to know that the Tower does not have a bell installed in its belfry; the bell that rings is actually installed on the roof of the Old Court House and is rung by means of a wire connected to the clock mechanism.

Opposite: The Prince of Wales Hotel, built in the late 1800s, and later named in honor of the Prince's visit to Canada, still welcomes visitors to the area.

Butler's Barracks

Several buildings were constructed on these grounds in the autumn of 1778 to relieve the severe overcrowding at Fort Niagara. They served as the nucleus for a new settlement by the Butler's Rangers and various Loyalist families at the end of the American Revolutionary War, 1783. Sometime before 1800 the buildings were destroyed by fire.

In 1814 British barracks and storehouses were rebuilt and named in memory of John Butler, a loyalist settler who commanded troops in the Seven Years War and the American Revolution. Butler's Barracks, built across the plain from Fort George, formed a military headquarters to guard an uneasy border after the War of 1812, and were a safe distance from the cannon fire of Fort Niagara. By 1854 there stood more than 20 buildings.

As the threat of war with the United States diminished, Butler's Barracks grew into a major training centre of the Canadian Army. Renamed Camp Niagara it served as a training centre for Canadians who served in the Boer War, the two World Wars and the Korean War. Both regulars and militia trained here until 1960. Today five original buildings have been restored from various periods.

Village of Queenston

Queenston was first known as West Landing, and later named after the Queen's Rangers by Lieutenant-Governor John Simcoe. Laura Secord lived here, Brock died here, and Mackenzie plotted to overthrow the government of his day from here.

Located at the head of navigation of the Niagara River, it was second only to Niagara as a shipping and trade centre. For Canada, Queenston was the terminal for the first primitive railroad. Horse-drawn carriages hauled goods to be portaged around the Falls to Chippewa to make their way to destinations further up the Great Lakes.

On October 13, 1812 the first major battle of the War of 1812 between Great Britain and the United States was fought here and on Queenston Heights. The day ended in a complete victory for the British and Canadian forces, but cost the life of General Brock.

A bridge link with the United States was proposed as early as 1836, and the first Queenston-Lewiston suspension bridge was opened March 18, 1851. A strong gale destroyed this bridge and the first structure was replaced in 1889. The present bridge was opened in 1962.

Up above the Village in a beautiful park stands a monument in memory of Major General Sir Isaac Brock.

Fort George

Fort George was built between 1796 and 1799 to replace Fort Niagara, located on the American side of the Niagara River, as the British Army Headquarters on the Niagara Frontier.

During the War of 1812, Fort George was occupied by American troops when a force of over 4000 American troops forced the British to retreat from Niagara. After the battle the Americans rebuilt the fort's defenses and during the rest of the summer and fall a 'guerilla war' was carried out against the Americans at the fort. By December 1813, the Americans were forced to leave Fort George which was then re-occupied by the British.

The fort was abandoned by the 1820s. The present works are a reconstruction done in 1937-40, and represent the fort as it was in 1799-1813. Only the magazine of the original fort remains.

Welland Ship Canal

The Welland Ship Canal was built as a direct access route for ships to travel from Lake Ontario to Lake Erie. Prior to the canal all freight had to be portaged from Queenston on the Niagara River to Chippawa Creek, so as to circumvent the Niagara Rapids and the dramatic fall of elevation at Niagara Falls.

Ships were towed through the 36 wooden lift locks that made up the first canal which was built in 1829. The difference in level between extreme low water levels of Lake Ontario and Lake Erie is 325.5 feet.

In all, four canals were built, each improving on the route, lock size, and materials used. The present canal, started in 1913, has 8 locks and is 25 miles long.

Ships in dry dock at the Port Weller Dry Docks on the Welland Canal.

White sails gleam in the summer sun on Lake Ontario.

A multitude of beautifully restored homes and public buildings, and a welcoming atmosphere combine to make Niagara-on-the-Lake a favorite stop for visitors in the summer. Tourism is one of the major industries for this area, but despite the annual influx of visitors, Niagara-on-the-Lake recreates the atmosphere of an earlier, gentler era.

The natural beauty and fine weather of Niagara also lends itself to outdoor pursuits. Cycling, sailing on the lake and exploring the mighty Niagara River are enjoyed by residents and visitors alike.

37

The Niagara-on-the-Lake Sailing Club

The Niagara Harbour and Dock Company, formed in 1831, undertook the task of filling in the marshland in front of the town. Excavation for the "slip", which was dug 18 feet lower than the river, was completed, as were a foundry and construction of a wharf. In 1848, 150-350 men were employed to build vessels, but the construction of the Welland Canal took its toll on Niagara as a commercial transportation centre. The company held on until the 1850s. Today it is a pleasure craft marina.

Agriculture in Niagara

In early May the trees of the Niagara fruitbelt burst into bloom. The majority of the Niagara Peninsula's fruitlands are located north of the Niagara Escarpment on the rich soil of the Lake Iroquois glacial plain which stretches to the shores of Lake Ontario. The Niagara Escarpment (250-300 ft. high) forms a ridge 3-7 miles away from the southern shores of Lake Ontario and shelters a section of the glacial plain. This serves as a protection for the farmlands from early frost in the fall and spring. This major fruit-growing region, which accounts for 90% of Ontario's total production, is the only area which can support the tender crops, because of a mild climate tempered by Lake Ontario.

Tree produce such as apples, cherries, peaches, pears and plums, to name a few, are shipped from here to all parts of Canada.

The Niagara area is also the "Grape and Wine Country", with a 1982 harvest of nearly 60,000 tons of grapes or 77% of Canada's total production.

These luscious bunches of grapes at the Niagara Vineyards will be used in the production of wine, one of the region's primary industries.

Fruit and vegetables, fresh picked, can be bought from numerous farmers' markets such as this.

Navy Hall

One of three or four rectangular wooden buildings, Navy Hall was constructed between 1775-1787 for use by the officers of the Naval Department serving on Lake Ontario.

Lieutenant-Governor Simcoe and his wife resided here in a building repaired July 1792. Distinguished visitors such as Prince Edward, fourth son of George III, Alexander MacKenzie, Joseph Brant and Duc de La Rochefoucault were entertained here.

This one building prepared for Parliament in 1792 was known as the Red Barracks and later used as a storehouse. The exact location of that September 17, 1792 inaugural meeting remains under dispute. Some historians claim the session was held under a large oak tree and others insist the setting was the Freemason's Hall.

By 1911 the building was almost in ruins and through a petition by the Niagara Historical Society the government restored Navy Hall in 1912. Covered by a stone facing, it was once a museum and it is now used by Parks Canada.

The Shaw Festival

The Shaw Festival began in 1962 when lawyer Brian Doherty organized performances of DON JUAN IN HELL and CANDIDA by George Bernard Shaw at the Court House on Queen St. A decade later on June 20, 1973 Queen Elizabeth II opened the new 860 seat Festival Theatre. Today the Shaw Festival, under the direction of Christopher Newton, as well as presenting Shavian plays, European farces and dramas in the Court House and Festival Theatre, offers musical comedies and lunchtime theatre at the recently acquired Royal George Playhouse.

The photograph opposite shows the Shaw Festival production of CYRANO DE BERGERAC by Edmond Rostand, translated and adapted by Anthony Burgess. Pictured left to right are Peter Krantz as De Valvert and Heath Lamberts as Cyrano de Bergerac.

Brock's Monument

This monument was erected in memory of Major-General Sir Isaac Brock, killed in action on the morning of October 13, 1812 in an attempt to retake the Heights from the Americans at Queenston. Brock, along with his aide-de-camp, Lieutenant-Colonel John MacDonell, who died in the second attempt to regain the Heights, were buried at the northeast bastion of Fort George.

Built to resemble a Tuscan monument, construction was begun in 1824. When the monument had reached a height of 48 feet, it was realized that William Lyon Mackenzie, a rebel political activist, had inserted a copy of the Colonial Advocate inside the cornerstone, and the column was ordered torn down, so as to remove the paper.

On April 17, 1840 Benjamin Lett, an Irish-Canadian rebel, destroyed the monument with a massive blast of gunpowder. The bodies were disinterred and buried in the nearby Hamilton cemetery, until the present monument begun in 1853 was completed, where they were finally laid to rest. Brock's monument stands 196 feet.

Opposite: The Shaw Festival Theatre.

Mackenzie House/The Colonial Advocate

The Colonial Advocate, an influential journal of radical reform was first published May 18, 1824, at Queenston, by William Lyon Mackenzie. A native of Scotland, Mackenzie had immigrated to Upper Canada in 1820 and three years later settled here and opened a general store. Within a year he had established a printing office in his home on this site, but in November 1824, moved to York (Toronto). Because of Mackenzie's frequent attacks on the "Family Compact" (the provincial administration and the group of persons who held most of Upper Canada's higher offices), supporters of this group raided the Colonial Advocate's offices and damaged the press on June 8, 1826. The courts awarded Mackenzie damages and he soon resumed publication. Mackenzie severed his connection with the paper, now called the Advocate, in 1834 and the last issue appeared that November. The constructed two-story residence was opened in 1938 by the rebel leader's grandson, Prime Minister William Lyon Mackenzie King.

McFarland House

 This gracious Georgian house, built in 1800 of handmade bricks, belonged to James McFarland on land purchased about 1795 by his father, John McFarland (1757-1814), who was described as "His Majesty's boat builder."

 Then one of Niagara district's finest residences, it was used during the War of 1812 as a hospital by both British and United States forces. A British battery was emplaced behind the house to command the river. In 1813 John McFarland was taken prisoner by the Americans following the capture of Fort George. When he returned in 1814, much of his property had been destroyed and the house badly damaged. It is now restored and furnished with Loyalist antiques.

Fort Mississauga

On the night of December 10, 1813 Fort George and the Old Town of Niagara was burned to the ground by retreating American forces. Bricks and rubble salvaged from the ruins of the Town were used in the construction of Fort Mississauga which was begun in 1814. Commanding the mouth of the Niagara River, Fort Mississauga, the only star-shaped fort in Canada, was to serve as a strategic defense for the area.

The central keep or tower, with its eight-foot thick walls, was the heart of the fortification. Two brick-lined powder magazines are located within the earthen walls, but they are earth filled to protect them from further deterioration, as is a sally port which led to the river's edge. The fort's outer buildings were constructed of wood and have long been demolished. Fort Mississauga was completed following the War of 1812 and was never attacked.

Autumn leaves blanket the ground at Field's Cemetery, along the Niagara Parkway.

Pear trees in brilliant fall colors.

Winter brings its own charm to Niagara-on-the-Lake, when fresh snow accents the houses and grounds, and hoarfrost lends nature's glitter to the scene.

St. Mark's Parish Hall and, opposite, the Breakenridge-Hawley House, circa 1818.

The Oban Inn

The Oban Inn is one of the oldest buildings in the Old Town of Niagara-on-the-Lake. Duncan Milloy, a lake captain from Oban, Scotland had this building built as his home in 1824. Captain Milloy purchased the Niagara Harbour and Dock Company and operated a transportation service from Toronto to Niagara.

Today the Oban Inn is one of the finer inns in Ontario, with almost two dozen rooms, no two alike.

St. Andrew's Presbyterian Church

The Presbyterians of Niagara had a Meeting House as early as 1792. The first church on this site was built in 1794. In 1813 it was burnt by invading troops of the United States as they retreated from Niagara. The present edifice, erected in 1831 by Cooper, a master builder/architect, is one of Ontario's finest examples of Greek Revival ecclesiastical architecture. The roof was remodeled in 1855 by Kivas Tully and the whole church was restored by architect Eric Arthur in 1937. The interior has been preserved in its original state and is one of the very few in Canada with high pulpit and box pews.

Opposite: The Bruce Trail, a 430-mile footpath which follows the Escarpment, through mostly wild and rugged country, from Niagara to Tobermory. Completed in 1967, the trail is for the most part on private land, with the consent of the owners.

Additional Photographic Credits

Michael Burch, Photo/Graphics: P. 30, 32. John Burridge, Photo/Graphics: P. 11. Fred Chapman, Photo/Graphics: P. 17. David Cooper: P. 47. J. A. Kraulis, Photo/Graphics: P. 36, 37, 49.